A DAY
AT THE
PARK

In Celebration of Wrigley Field

Revised Edition

By William Hartel

Foreword by George Will

Quality Sports Publications

Cover and dustjacket designed by
Mick McCay

PHOTOGRAPHERS

Mary Butkus
Jennifer Chambers
Roberta Devlin
Lynn DuBard
Kenneth Fanti
Ray Foli
Cliff Gokenbach
William Greenblatt
Michael Gustafson
Daniel Hartel
Laura Jarnow
Kathy Swartzbaugh
Laura Swartzbaugh
Marc Swartzbaugh
Margie Swartzbaugh
Alison Whelan
Timothy Wingert

For information write:

Quality Sports Publications
P.O. Box 6278
Rock Island, IL 61204-6278
(800) 464-1116

Duane Brown, Project Director
Melinda Brown, Designer
Susan Smith, Editor

Printed in the U.S.A
by
Walsworth Publishing Company

ISBN 1-885758-03-0

To the Memory of My Loving Father, Frank Hartel

"Perhaps there have been those who have scoffed at Mr. Wrigley's vine-covered outfield wall, his terraced bleachers with the Chinese elms. Perhaps some have wondered that the largest pre-war buyer of advertising signboards has no signboards in his ball park. Perhaps others have thought him foolish for throwing out hundreds of chairs to install wider and more comfortable ones...(but) there is overwhelming evidence that Mr. Wrigley's foresight in demanding neatness, comfort and beauty as an essential (and profitable) adjunct of baseball entertainment has proven a grand success. The success will be even more apparent when those responsible are able to again assemble a winning team..."

– The Sporting News, 1944

Contents

Acknowledgments

I would like to thank my photographers, as much for their hard work as for their trust in me and the project. Their skill and dedication turned my vision into a reality. Special thanks to Michael Gustafson and Omniflight Helicopters for their outstanding aerial work. And thanks also to Kodak for supplying the film for this project.

I am grateful to all of the contributors for sharing their memories of the beautiful ballpark, and to those writers who permitted me to reprint from their work.

Thanks to *The Sporting News* in St. Louis and the National Baseball Library in Cooperstown for opening their archives and assisting me in the historical research. And thanks to the Chicago Historical Society for agreeing to preserve in their archives the collection of more than 3,000 different photos taken for the book so that future generations can relive a day at Wrigley Field back in 1993.

I am indebted to Eddie Gold of the *Chicago Sun Times* who reviewed much of the manuscript for accuracy, to Sam Pathy who provided several of the photo captions, and to Raymond Kush for sharing some of his highly detailed research material. And special thanks to Skip Rozin, an excellent writer and builder of confidence.

The Society for American Baseball Research (SABR) provided assistance throughout the project. SABR is a remarkable organization made up of helpful and friendly people dedicated to researching all the aspects of the game of baseball.

Secretarial assistance was provided by Beth Schnaak who can, in fact, type faster than I can read. And for extraordinary effort in getting everyone to Chicago, coordinating the busy day of photography, and editing *way* too many slides and photos, my thanks to Ann Friend.

And the most heartfelt thanks to my wife, Alison Whelan, whose encouragement kept the project alive, even as powerful thunderstorms enveloped Chicago in the early dawn hours of June 18. You are my inspiration.

Preface

Wrigley Field was a sort of heaven of my youth: the El trip to the park, without parental supervision, was high adventure. The walk to the bleacher gates from the Addison stop was long for my little Keds, but the neighborhood always pulsed with pre-game excitement: I felt swept away in a stream of blue-clad fans as we flowed through the gates. Hot dogs and popcorn were the food of gods. Although I carefully kept score and hung on every pitch, what mattered more to me than the score was that I was sitting in the bleachers and watching baseball. I would return home slightly crisped from my afternoon in the sun, tired from the excitement of the day, yet exhilarated. This was the great stuff of life.

Most magical places of childhood are best left as memories and not re-visited. So often, when the child returns with adult eyes and attitudes, the place is older and worn; its dimensions have diminished; the shine has faded, and the magic that was once there disappears forever. But Wrigley Field has retained its special magic. I have returned to the park often as an adult. I have even ridden the El as the unwanted parent shepherding my young children to the ballpark. The park has shrunken as I have grown: I now stroll easily all the way around the park, and often do before a game, and now I can afford the "good" seats should I choose. I notice things that I missed as a child -- faded paint, rusted support beams, long lines -- yet the magic remains.

I often wonder how the passage of time that tarnishes my other childhood memories creates such a rich patina for Wrigley Field.

What is the essence of the park and the nature of its attraction? It's not the Cubs -- ball players come and go, as the back of my old baseball cards can attest, and even whole teams pick up and move. It is partly Wrigley's quaintness -- the hand-operated scoreboard, the alluring ivy. The park today is much like it was for my grandparents. And it is partially the ballpark community -- friendly and pleasant. But Wrigley Field is also about tradition, aging gracefully, green grass, and fitting in with your neighbors.

The tremendous appeal of Wrigley Field is not just that it is the home to the Chicago Cubs, although that is what made it special for me as a child. It also is loved for its place in history, its place in the neighborhood, and its place in the heart of the people who come to take in the game... to watch the Cubs... but mostly who come to enjoy *A Day at the Park....*

All of the color photos in this book were taken in and around Wrigley Field on Friday, June 18, 1993. Among the many things that happened there that day, the Chicago Cubs played a baseball game against the Cardinals of St. Louis.

W.J.H.

Foreword

By George F. Will
Syndicated Columnist
1976 Pulitzer Prize Winner
Author, *Men at Work*

Toward the Corner of Clark and Addison

The first time I went to Europe I traveled by ship. A good thing, that. It meant that I did not first set foot in the Old World in the antiseptic glass and stainless steel corridors of an airport that could as well be in Los Angeles as London. Rather, I stepped into England through the old port of Southampton, and so experienced with full force a particularly American wonderment: How many shoes have trod upon these stones? And if these stones could speak, how many generations would they speak of?

Now, ask yourself this. Where, here at home, can we Americans have a similar sensation of mingling with the shades of many generations? In a few of the older neighborhoods of our older cities, neighborhoods that have eluded the heavy tread of Progress and not been transformed many times. And perhaps in some rural communities, particularly out West. But it is a lovely fact, and one that speaks volumes about the interweaving of the national pastime with the national experience, that we can experience the sense of mingling with the generations -- the almost palpable presence of the past -- in a few ballparks. And nowhere more than in Wrigley Field.

In Wrigley Field's first 79 years, through 1993, about 85 million people have attended baseball games there. That is a crowd not much smaller than the population of the United States (99 million) in 1914, when what is now known as Wrigley Field was brand spanking new.

If grandparents brought grandchildren to the park in 1914, as surely some did, then there may today be some seventh generation Cubs fans in the grandstands. A grandfather in 1914 could have been a Civil War veteran. And a youngster in the Wrigley Field bleachers today may bring grandchildren here when this nation celebrates its Tricentennial in the year 2076.

Wrigley Field, so saturated with memories, is cherished by a nation too often enamored of novelty. The nation, or at least its baseball fans, may have learned a stern lesson. As someone -- Oscar Wilde, I think -- once warned, people should be careful not to be too modern; they run the risk of quite suddenly seeming old-fashioned. Fans in Philadelphia, Cincinnati, Pittsburgh, Atlanta, Oakland, San Diego and St. Louis can ruefully confirm that.

Not long ago they were given up-to-date, state-of-the-art "multipurpose" stadiums. And today those stadiums look like young relics -- like bellbottom slacks and platform shoes. Or perhaps even more like another fad from the silly Seventies, the Pet Rock.

These misbegotten stadiums were designed to accommodate both baseball and football, which makes about as much sense as designing a building to be both a library and a foundry. The question of the proper setting for watching a football game seems to me utterly unimportant. I mean, how important is the venue of trainwreck?

Football should be watched, if at all, on television, so the camera can bring the spectator close enough to the carnage to make sense of the piles of bodies. But baseball, the most observable of team sports, with the players widely dispersed on eye-pleasing green, should be played as close to the observant fans as possible -- so close that even fans far back in the stands can hear the infielders' chatter. Cub fans can hear it.

The people who perpetrated the "multipurpose" edifices forgot a fundamental principle of design, the principle that explains the beauty of, for example, the old clipper ships. The principle is that function should dictate form. That simple notion explains the timeless beauty of, and unfailing satisfaction given by, Wrigley Field and a few other old parks.

When the state of Maryland built Oriole Park at Camden Yards in Baltimore, it aimed not to break new ground but to recapture lost ground. And the resounding success of Camden Yards is confirmed every time a fan exclaims, "It reminds me of Wrigley Field!"

With the new parks built in Cleveland and Texas, baseball's quest continues, the quest to capture at least a portion of the perfection that Cub fans rightly consider their birthright. It is altogether proper that as baseball ends the long detour that took it away from its best architectural heritage, baseball finds itself striding, as it were, toward the corner of Clark and Addison.

An aerial view of the corner of Clark and Addison, the morning of June 18, 1993.

The corner of Waveland and Sheffield, 1932. This is the way the park looked when
Babe Ruth "called" his shot during the 1932 World Series.

Once Upon A Time

By William Hartel

Waveland and Sheffield... Those names go together like baseball and hot dogs. Sports fans the world over can tell you that those are the streets that define the outfield at Chicago's Wrigley Field. It's hard to imagine professional baseball without the Cubs, and perhaps even harder to imagine Chicago without Wrigley Field. The ballpark is such a perfect place to watch a game that it seems it must be the result of careful and thoughtful long-range planning by Mr. Wrigley; but its very existence today is as much a product of luck and happenstance.

In the late 1830s, Chicago was *the* place to be. The region (in those days it couldn't be called a "city" by any stretch) was like a gangly, unruly adolescent, just embarking on a period of unprecedented growth and development. The land by the Great Lake, recently acquired from indians, was attracting investors and land speculators in droves, including 44-year-old Joseph Sheffield, a native of Connecticut. Sheffield, who had spent many years in Mobile, Alabama, as a cotton exporter, moved to Chicago to establish a nursery. By the late 1840s, the game of baseball had become popular with youngsters, and Sheffield's business

interests had diversified. By the mid-1850s, Sheffield had founded the Chicago, Rock Island and Pacific Railroad, and was developing the area north of Chicago which would later be known as Lake View.

Sheffield reinvested in the neighborhood, buying up the land adjacent to Clark Avenue. As was customary, he gave one of the streets his family name, Sheffield Avenue. When he saw that much of his land was submerged by nearby Lake Michigan during bad weather, the successful businessman showed a sense of humor by choosing the name "Waveland" for a road which crossed the street that bore his name, creating the intersection of Waveland and Sheffield Avenues.

But baseball at that now-famous intersection was still a long way off. Chicago was ravaged by its Great Fire in 1871, prompting city officials to modify building codes to prevent another such disaster. Wooden frame buildings, which had been the main fuel for the fire, were prohibited within the city limits. Businesses, faced not only with the cost of rebuilding their factories and offices, but now rebuilding them with more costly masonry, began to search the surrounding area for cheaper land and less strict building codes. Sheffield's Lake

View area, outside the city limits at the time, looked very attractive.

At the time of the Chicago Fire, professional baseball was in its infancy. Baseball back then was played like softball today, no gloves and underhand pitching. Less attention was paid to the rules than to having fun. But the White Stockings, Chicago's pro team, were good, and they were in a three-way battle for the championship when the great fire burned down their wooden grandstand at Michigan Avenue and Randolf Street. The team, forced to play their final games in other parks with loaned equipment, lost to the Athletics of Philadelphia.

In 1874, a few years after the famous fire and a few years before the National League of Professional Baseball Clubs was founded, Lutheran minister William Passavant inherited several acres of a sandy grove north of Chicago, populated only by cottonwoods and ash trees. The missionary, who was spreading his faith from Nova Scotia to Nebraska, immediately donated the land to the Lutherans with the intention of establishing a church and school on the property. He built St. Mark's Lutheran Church, and introduced Chicagoans to Lutheran conservatism. 1874 was also the year that Charles Henry Weeghman, "Lucky Charlie" as he would later be known, was born in Indiana.

In 1891, Passavant opened the Theological Seminary of the Evangelical Lutheran Church with six students; meanwhile, the interest in pro baseball was sweeping the city and the nation. According to

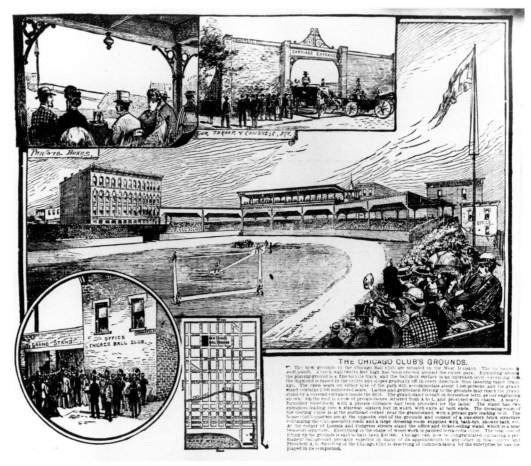

West Side Park was used by the White Stockings from 1885 to 1892. The team was also known as the Colts when they played there. They were evicted so the ground could be used for the Columbian Exposition of 1893. The park was located at what is today the intersection of Harrison Street and Throop Street. *Photo credit National Baseball Library and Archive, Cooperstown, NY.*

THE CHICAGO CLUB'S GROUNDS.

Weeghman Park, Home of the Federal League Whales, 1914. *Photo credit National Baseball Library and Archive, Cooperstown, NY.*

the *Chicago Tribune* at the time, "Chicago is a city of baseball maniacs."

Chicago's professional baseball team used many nicknames in the 1890s, including the Broncos and the Colts. When their long-time manager "Cap" Anson was replaced in 1898, the Colts became known as the Orphans, when the American League, formed in 1901, raided their ranks, the Orphans became the Remnants. During this decade, businesses and industry moved into the Lake View area to take advantage of proximity to the Milwaukee Road rail yard. Also during the decade, Chicago's public transportation network was developing; by the turn of the century, the elevated train line that now runs by Wrigley Field was in use, as was the Clark Street trolley.

By 1908, Chicago's National League team had settled on the name "Cubs," and they were also World Champions, playing winning baseball at the West Side Grounds at Taylor Street and Lincoln Avenue (now Wolcott Street), which seated 16,000

in a double-decked grandstand. In the Lake View area, which was now part of Chicago, business was booming, and the Milwaukee Road rail yards, a block or so from the seminary, were busier than ever. The hustle and bustle bothered Lutheran church officials, who purchased some of the property at the intersection of Clark and Addison adjacent to church grounds with the hopes of establishing a buffer zone around the school to ensure a tranquil environment for the students.

The Cubs had another good year in 1910, winning their fourth pennant in five years at their West Side location. Professional baseball was also having a banner year, as national attendance topped seven million, and Comiskey Park, "Baseball Palace of the World," opened on Chicago's South Side.

It was also a busy year for business in the Lake View region. Industry continued to grow, and with it came more noise and nuisance that was not conducive to religious study. As the popularity of the region increased, so did the land values. Church

While under construction, 490 men worked on the project – 350 on the structure itself, and 140 on the landscaping. The entire construction required just seven weeks, including a two-day work stoppage by striking union workers. Original building permit for Weeghman Park. *From the collection of Raymond Kush. (© William Hartel, 1993.)*

DEPARTMENT OF BUILDINGS

CITY OF CHICAGO

CITY HALL

APPLICATION FOR BUILDING PERMIT

March 5th 191_8_

Commissioner of Buildings,

    City of Chicago.

Dear Sir–

    Application is hereby made for permit and use of water for building to be erected on

Lot...... *Entire* Block *14 of Laflin Smith & Dyer Subdivision of the N.E. 1/4 (except 1.28 acres in N.E. Corner) of Sec 20 T. 40 NR 14. E*

Street and Number... *1000 & 1052 Addison St. & 3601 to 3605 N. Clark St.*

Owner *Chicago Federal League* Address *1052 Addison St.*

Architect *Zachary C. & Charles G. Davis* Address *Steinway Hall Chicago*

Mason Contractor *Blome Sinek Co* Address *City Hall Square Bldg*

Carpenter Contractor... *do* ...Address... *do*

Use to which buildings will be put *Grand Stand* No. of Stories *One*

Length *800* Breadth *100* Height *56* Brick or Frame *Stel & Concrete*

Number of Brick *160 m* Number of Cords of Stone————

Number of Cubic Feet of Concrete *45200* Number of Cubic Feet of Hollow Tile *1900*

No. of Yds. of Plastering *1700*

Total Cost of Building... *$250 000*

Remarks:...

....

....

....

The applicant hereby certifies to the correctness of the above.

Signature *Blome Sinek Co*

Address *City Hall Square Bldg*

officials were offered $175,000 by Milwaukee investor Charles Havenor for their property, far more than its assessed value. Fearing that the area around the church grounds could never return to its quiet beginnings, they grabbed the money and ran.

The seminary closed its doors and moved to Maywood, far away from "the smoke, dust, grime, soot, dirt... (and the) ding-donging of bells late and early" that accompanied the busy railroad yards across the street. Havenor planned to make his money on the property by leasing the land to the railroad for switching trains.

The two established professional baseball organizations, the National and the American Leagues, were becoming powerhouses. There was money to be made in owning and operating a professional baseball team, and a group of investors formed the Federal Baseball League in the winter of 1912. Chicago's team in the new league, the

Chicago Whales' Opening Day, 1915, at Weeghman Park. The Cubs moved to the park the following year after the Federal League folded. Note how little the apartment buildings beyond left field have changed since the ballpark was built. The Whales dugout is along the third base side of the playing field, the same side occupied by the Cubs today.

Looking west on Addison Street at Weeghman Park, 1915. When it opened to the public in April 1914, Weeghman Park was a single-level steel and concrete structure seating 14,000 fans. *Photo credit Chicago Historical Society.*

Weeghman Park at the end of the 1915 season. The Whales were playing for the League Championship, which they won by a fraction of a percentage point. The small section on the roof behind home plate served as the press-box. *Photo credit Chicago Historical Society.*

ChiFeds, played their 1913 season at the DePaul University athletic field.

In August 1913, Federal League founders raised their sights to the level of the established major leagues, and convinced a handful of "big wheels" to invest in their league and attempt to compete with the National and American Leagues.

Charles Weeghman, who came to Chicago as a waiter in 1892, had made millions of dollars in the restaurant business. An avid sports fan, he had tried several times to purchase Chicago's National League team with his riches, without success. With the formation of a third major league, Weeghman finally had his chance to run a ball team. He bought the ChiFeds with William Walker, a fish distributor.

In the winter of 1913, Weeghman was named president of the club, and set out to build a place to play. In his effort to legitimize his team and the new league, Weeghman wanted more than just a ball field -- he wanted to give Chicagoans "a park which will outshine any other in either the National or American Leagues, with the exception of the one at the Polo Grounds in New York."

On December 31, 1913, Weeghman signed a deal to lease the property at Clark and Addison for 99 years with Edmund Archambault, who had acquired the land in pieces over the years from

Havenor. The lease, which cost Weeghman $16,000 per year, specified that Weeghman had to build modern buildings on the land, that the land could not be used for "immoral or illegal purposes," and that the cost of the improvements could not exceed $70,000. He hired architect Zachary Taylor Davis, the designer of Comiskey Park, to plan and build his park.

Work on his Federal League ballpark began immediately. Four wooden Seminary buildings were torn down February 23, 1914, and the ground was

broken the following week in front of more than 5,000 spectators. Whether Weeghman secretly intended to violate the terms of his lease when he signed it we will never know, but within two short months he had plowed a quarter of a million dollars into the property, three times the limit specified in the contract. On April 23, 1914, he opened his park to an appreciative standing-room-only audience of 21,000, as his ChiFeds took on the Kansas City Packers. Meanwhile, the Cubs, who were no longer playing up to their former winning ways, drew just

Opening Day, 1917, the Cubs' second season at Weeghman Park. The troops were on the field for the pre-game festivities to bolster support for the country as it entered World War I. *Photo credit National Baseball Library and Archive, Cooperstown, NY.*

4,000 on their opening day at the West Side Grounds.

During their first three games at Weeghman Park, the ChiFeds hit nine homers over the short left-field fence. While the team was on its first road trip, Weeghman had workers move the left field fence back 25 feet, which required demolishing the front of a house on Waveland Avenue.

Weeghman was always aware of the value of a little publicity, so in 1915 he sponsored a "name the team" contest. The nickname "Whales" was selected out of 350 entries, although no one is quite sure why. Weeghman also initiated a "Ladies Day," which increased the team's appeal -- the National League had outlawed such a promotion in a 1901 ruling. Cubs' attendance was falling as the team dropped below .500, and the fans shifted allegiance to the first-place Whales, who captured the Federal League Championship that year, or the second-place American League White Sox.

The Whales were on a roll, but the Federal League was not, and the League folded at the conclusion of the 1915 season. As a condition of the settlement with the older leagues, two Federal League team owners were permitted to buy into the established leagues. St. Louis ice machine manufacturer Phil Ball purchased the St. Louis Browns, and Weeghman was permitted to buy

Opposite page: Wrigley Field circa 1920. By this time, Weeghman was broke and his Chicago restaurant chain had been handed over to creditors. His ballfield had been renamed "Cubs Park," and he was out of baseball for good. The right-field fence shown here is a short 298 feet. *Photo credit the National Baseball Library and Archive, Cooperstown, NY.*

Upper: In 1922, Wrigley hired Zachary Davis, the ballpark's original architect, to design and coordinate extensive modifications. Eleven sections behind home plate were placed on rollers and moved 60 feet toward the intersection of Clark and Addison. Likewise, 11 sections of the left-field grandstands were rolled 60 feet toward Waveland Avenue. The right-field stands, pictured above, were left in place. The playing field was lowered three feet to improve the view, and new box seats were installed for fan comfort. The remodeling cost $300,000 – more than the entire cost of building the park just eight years earlier. *Photo credit National Baseball Library and Archive, Cooperstown, NY.*

The bleachers, constructed in 1923, originally extended from foul pole to foul pole. In 1925, the right-field bleachers were removed with the exception of the small "jury box" grandstand seen here. The Wrigley Doublemint Twins are mounted atop the scoreboard. *Photo credit National Baseball Library and Archive, Cooperstown, NY.*

controlling interest in the Cubs. He put together a group of 10 investors, including chewing gum magnate William Wrigley, and bought the team from Charles Taft, half brother of the former president for $500,000.

In his first official act as Cubs president, Weeghman folded his Whales into the Cubs and move the team to his park at Clark and Addison, Waveland and Sheffield, where they opened the 1916 season on April 20 with a win over the Reds, 7 to 6.

Weeghman not only moved the Cubs to his ballpark on the North Side -- he brought with them Pat Pieper as the field announcer. Pieper became a fixture in the park, where he would announce the starting lineups for the next six decades.

In August, Weeghman announced that he would allow fans to keep balls batted into the stands, which started a trend among team owners and made him popular with the fans. Prior to that, balls hit into the crowd had to be retrieved and returned to the playing field.

Although his innovations increased fan support, the team was not performing well, finishing in fifth place two years in a row. His other investments weren't performing well either, and the waiter-turned-millionaire, strapped for cash, sold off shares of the team to Wrigley. By 1918, the Cubs had turned it around, finishing an impressive 40 games over .500, but Weeghman was broke, and was forced to sell his remaining interest in the team to Wrigley.

The Cubs took the National League title that year, but lost the World Series to the Boston Red Sox and their young pitcher, Babe Ruth. The Series was played at cross-town Comiskey Park, which held twice the capacity of Weeghman Park.

The Cubs' home field became known as "Cubs Park" by 1920, and the Chicago Bears football team took up residence there following the 1921 baseball season. The following year Wrigley hired Zachary Davis, the park's original architect, to design and direct a massive remodeling project. The grandstand sections behind home plate and left field were placed on rollers and were moved to enlarge the playing field and create room for additional seating. The modifications, which cost more than the entire park had cost to build, increased the seating capacity to 20,000. When the 1923 season opened, the playing field dimensions were 325 feet to left, 318 feet to right, and the park's longest dimension ever, 447 feet to center.

In 1924, Wrigley purchased the land and the ball park, and two years later, the park was officially renamed Wrigley Field. Almost immediately, people began referring to it as "Beautiful Wrigley Field," especially during the regular radio broadcasts of the games. Wrigley placed renewed emphasis on the team, signing tough Joe McCarthy as manager and announcing plans to add a second deck to his park. In 1927, the second deck over the left-field grandstands was completed, which helped boost attendance to 1.2 million, making the Cubs the first team to pass the million mark. The following year, the remainder of the park was double-decked, increasing the capacity to just under 40,000.

1932 marked two milestones in the history of Wrigley Field. The first was the death of William Wrigley at age 70, passing control of the team and the ballpark to his son, Philip. The second was the legendary "called shot" by Babe Ruth during the 1932 World Series. Whether the Babe actually pointed to the spot where he hit his famous homer is widely debated, but Curtis Candy, the makers of the Baby Ruth candy bar, erected a monument to the home run that stood for decades -- a lighted "Baby Ruth" sign atop an apartment building on Sheffield Avenue overlooking the right-center field bleachers where the Babe's home run landed.

The left-field stands were double-decked in 1927. This helped boost the Cubs' attendance that year to over one million, making them the first team to achieve this milestone. *Photo credit National Baseball Library and Archive, Cooperstown, NY.*

The rest of the park was double-decked in 1928. This is the way the park looked when P.K. Wrigley became owner of the team after William died at age 70. *Photo credit National Baseball Library and Archive, Cooperstown, NY.*

The Cubs of the 1930s were a powerful team, playing in three World Series in the decade. P.K. Wrigley had announced plans to substantially remodel the park, which by then was almost a quarter-century old. Construction on the new outfield and scoreboard began in July, with the team way out in first place and looking like they would go all the way again. The 150-man construction crew started work early every morning so they could wrap up the day's activities an hour or so before game time. The dili-gent work paid off, and the remodeling was finished by September -- unfortunately so was the team, fin-ishing behind the New York Giants.

The construction of the bleachers and scoreboard was the last major change in the park's configuration. The field dimensions, 353 feet to right field, 400 feet to center and 355 feet (and seven inches, according to the *Chicago Tribune* in 1938) to left field, remain unchanged.

The West Side Grounds, the only place that

was ever home to the "World Champion Chicago Cubs," was torn down after the team moved to Weeghman Park. Today on that spot stands the University of Illinois Medical Center. The Lutheran Seminary, which was razed to make room for Weeghman's ballpark, moved from Maywood to the scholarly neighborhood of Hyde Park in the mid-1980s, where they expect to be for a long time.

For more than 80 years, the land at Clark and Addison, Waveland and Sheffield has been home to professional baseball. If the engineers and architects who thoroughly inspected the park in 1989 are correct, baseball can continue to be enjoyed there for at least another 80 years.

This was the park's configuration in 1936, the last year that Wrigley Field went without left-field bleachers. The following year, the entire outfield area was rebuilt into the configuration used today. *Photo Credit The Sporting News*

Wrigley Field, circa 1938. The outfield area, bleachers and scoreboard were constructed in 1937. P.K. Wrigley wanted an "outdoorsy motif" for the new bleachers and had full-grown elm trees planted on concrete steps behind the bleacher seats. Four of the trees can be seen in this aerial photo to the left of the scoreboard. As you can see, fans were permitted to sit in the center-field area of the bleachers. Newspaper accounts in 1938 reported the value of the property and ballpark to be $3 million (not including the team). *Photo credit* The Sporting News.

Below is Wrigley Field following the outfield construction. The capacity of the park during the 1938 season was 37,500. For the World Series that year, the capacity was increased to 47,000 by the addition of almost 10,000 small folding chairs. *Photo credit* The Sporting News.

Upper photo: The outside of the scoreboard as it looked in 1938, the year it was completed. The tradition of hanging flags representing the division standings was initiated that year. *Photo credit* The Sporting News.

Lower photo: Addison Street was widened following the 1939 season. This is the right-field corner of the field. The octagonal section near the bottom of the scoreboard is the football quarter clock. The clock atop the scoreboard was not added for several years. *Photo credit* The Sporting News.

Upper photo: The back of the scoreboard, 1945. Compare this to the earlier photo of the scoreboard, and you will see that the elm trees have been removed. This was the year the face of the scoreboard and the bleacher seats were painted the green color they are today. The outfield area, the bleachers and the face of the scoreboard were originally reddish-brown. *Photo credit National Baseball Library and Archive, Cooperstown, NY.*

Lower photo: The outfield area late in the 1951 season. The center-field section, known as "hitter's background," was open to bleacher fans from 1937 through the 1940 season, and was closed to fans from 1941 through 1950. The section was reopened in 1951, but was closed for good in 1952. Players had complained to the Commissioner of Baseball for years that they could not distinguish the ball in flight from the background of white-shirted fans in the outfield. *Photo credit The Sporting News.*

Wrigley Field during the 1962 All-Star game, the second one played that year. If you look very carefully, you can see six umpires on the playing field. In 1969, when the National League was expanded, the flagpole above the scoreboard was lengthened to accommodate the additional teams. This photo also shows how the park looked the first time professional baseball was ever telecast by satellite. Ninety seconds of a Cubs-Phillies game July 23, 1962, was beamed around the world on the Telstar network. *Photo credit National Baseball Library and Archive, Cooperstown, NY.*

"Wrigley Field: A Baseball Park That Radiates Joy"

By Paul Goldberger, *New York Times*

September 18, 1988
Copyright © by The New York Times Company. Reprinted by permission.

It is not within the power of architecture to guarantee that we have a good time -- except, perhaps, at Wrigley Field. For this extraordinary baseball park, this amiable pile of steel and concrete that despite careful maintenance still shows every one of its 74 years, seems to radiate more joy than all the domed stadiums of the last generation put together. The happiness in this place is palpable -- and it comes not merely from hometown loyalty to the Chicago Cubs, potent though that may be. The glow that envelopes Wrigley Field each time a game begins is, at bottom, a shared sense that there is basic rightness to this place, that it is a field full of grass in the middle of a city, one of the only places left in professional sports in which a game can be experienced more or less as it was half a century ago.

To be in Wrigley Field is to celebrate baseball as it once was -- and to discover the startling ability of a piece of architecture to evoke that time with easy grace. Wrigley Field is a place that is innocent of instant replay, of vast electronic scoreboards as cluttered with advertising as Times Square, of baseball as a business. It actually has the power to bring you back to a moment when the phrase "ball club" was not an oxymoron.

All of this has been so for some time, of course, but it is worth remarking that it is still true, in this, the year of Wrigley Field's much debated nighttime lighting. Last month the first night games in Wrigley Field's history were played, and there were great fears that with the installation of lights this ballpark would be finished, over, that it would become just like anyplace else. Not at all. First, the lighting fixtures themselves are fairly unobtrusive, and keep the stadium's integrity, such as it is, intact. But even a less modest installation could not destroy the things that make Wrigley Field one of the most beloved athletic facilities in the country: its size, its layout, and its relationship to the city of which it is utterly and totally a part.

Most sports facilities today are essentially interchangeable -- is there anything that speaks of New Orleans in the Superdome, of New York or New Jersey in Giants Stadium, of Seattle in the Kingdome? The Superdome, in fact, emerged quite directly out of the desire of New Orleans officials to give their city a bit of the allure of Houston, a pursuit in which they can be said to have succeeded admirably. Like convention centers, most sports facilities now are vast and anonymous, virtually identical from city to city, and altogether unrelated to the places into which they have been dropped.

Wrigley, by contrast, is small and open and

eccentric. It is of its place and for its place, which happens to be the corner of Addison and Clark Streets on the North Side. That address itself tells us much -- Wrigley Field is actually on a street, in a city; it is not some concrete whale in an ocean of parking lots. The elevated train rumbles by, there are sports-oriented bars on the corners facing the stadium gates, and the streets opposite the stadium are lined with houses whose upper floors offer a peek into the outfield. The structure is topped off with banners, and they signal whether the Cubs have won or lost. Anywhere else, this would seem a sentimental, even trite, gesture, but here it seems as natural as the bright red sign on the front that proudly proclaims "Wrigley Field Home of the Chicago Cubs" or the manual scoreboard or the presence of real, true grass.

It is easy to think of the appeal of all of this as merely a matter of nostalgia, and surely nostalgia is part of it. But there is something much deeper to Wrigley Field that is not a question of nostalgia at all, and that is the whole relationship this park engenders between fan and field, between player and fan, and between both of them and the city. In each case, the relationship has an intimacy that is completely lacking in larger, newer sports facilities. Because Wrigley Field is small -- its capacity is slightly over 39,000 -- no one is too far away from the field. From high up in the grand-stand, the diamond is a perfect panorama, and there is a wonderful view of Chicago to boot, yet there is still a feeling of being in touch; it is not like looking through the wrong end of a telescope, as the upper-level seats feel like in most stadiums. And from every seat, the grass of the field, with its celebrated wall of ivy behind it, is the benign central presence.

In some ways, with its exposed metal structure and plain, unadorned brick and concrete, Wrigley Field has more of a kinship with a structure like the Cyclone at Coney Island than with most sports stadiums. Like the roller coaster, it is a matter-of-fact and industrial structure on which time and use have conferred tremendous romantic power. Both structures have no unnecessary embellishments; they are stripped-down, functional objects, rising over residential neighborhoods, and over the years the architecture of each has become inextricably intertwined with cultural symbolism.

The ability of Wrigley Field to stand as a symbol raises the whole question of intention in romantic imagery. Did its makers intend this stadium to embody the classic imagery as a fully as it does? Probably not, given how simple and basic this building is; more likely, they were thinking only of easy, comfortable views of the playing field and of efficient movement of crowds. Wrigley Field's stature as a romantic object has gained gradually over the years, and comes in part by default; Ebbets Field, which possessed many similar virtues, is of course long gone, and Fenway Park in Boston is probably its only true peer.

But in this age of near-total obsession with applied romantic imagery -- this age of much architectural artifice, this age of Philip Johnson selling romantic imagery wholesale and Ralph Lauren selling it retail -- perhaps the real issue is the ability of this blunt, almost harsh building to evoke the pleasure of the past so convincingly. There is nothing about Wrigley Field that fits our age of excess. It is sparse, not ornate, and the only lush thing about it is the grass and the ivy.

Much of its appeal is a matter of authenticity, of course -- Wrigley Field is the real thing, and its realness shines through in an age of replication. But there may also be a lesson about accommodation in this building. Wrigley Field is not a dogmatic structure, or a forbidding one; it may be rough, but it is never mean or arbitrary. Indeed, in its shape, its orientation, its layout, its very architectural essence is accommodation -- accommodation to the fans, to the players, to the city and, above all, to the game of baseball.

"From high up in the grandstands, the diamond is a perfect panorama, and there is a wonderful view of Chicago to boot..."
– Paul Goldberger
The New York Times

"In some ways, with its exposed metal structure and plain, unadorned brick and concrete, Wrigley Field has more of a kinship with a structure like the Cyclone at Coney Island than with most sports stadiums... Both structures have no unnecessary embellishments; they are stripped-down, functional objects rising over residential neighborhoods, and over the years the architecture of each has become inextricably intertwined with cultural symbolism."
– Paul Goldberger
The New York Times

"*Wrigley is like another home in the community -- when you're in Wrigley Field it's like you're visiting the family of all the people that live around there.*"
— **Ernie Banks**
Cubs infielder, 1953-71

"It is no longer a glamour girl; paint cannot cover its cracks of age. Its history is long enough that players played here that my father could not have seen. Wrigley Field is an old summer home, full of warmth, beauty, green, tradition, cycles, homers, bad calls, memories and truth."

— Mike Bilski

"Baseball, as I have sometimes suggested, is above all a matter of belonging, and belonging to the Cubs takes a lifetime. But to Chicago, the Cubs are something more that just a team. Wrigley Field is almost the last of the old neighborhood parks, and the antiquity of the place... reminds us of what the game once felt like and how it fitted in to the patterns of city life."
— **Roger Angell**
Season Ticket

"I detest the appearance and flavor of most modern ballparks, which seem to have sprung from the same architectural tradition that brought us the shopping mall."
– Roger Angell
Five Seasons

"The ballpark is so often referred to as 'Beautiful Wrigley Field,' that some people believe the word 'Beautiful' is actually part of its official name."
– Judge Richard L.
   Curry

Memorandum Opinion 3/85 following Chicago National League Ball Club, Inc. vs State of Illinois and Lake View Citizen Council

When needed, the ground crew can get the tarp down in 55 seconds. It takes a bit longer to remove it from the playing field.

"Lines rising and falling in perfect harmony, set off by brilliant colors: The lush green of the grass, a mixture of five strains from Kentucky to protect against blight; the brownish-red of the base paths, pitcher's mound, batting area, a blend of sand and clay from New Jersey. Unlike many of the new sports facilities, where sections of yellow and blue and orange seats are keyed to ticket prices, all of Wrigley's seats are green, because parks are supposed to be green."
— **Skip Rozin**
Audubon, 1984

"Wrigley Field may be the best-loved park in baseball. If that's so, it's easy enough to understand why. In practically all of its magnificently maintained details, this place is a classic."
– Dan and Kieran Dickinson
Major League Stadiums, 1991

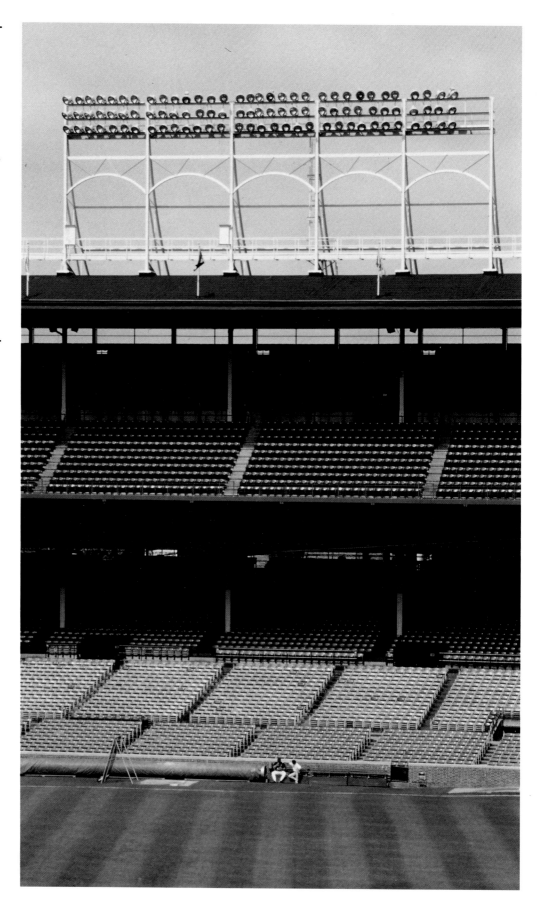

"Wrigley Field is a classic Midwestern cross between penurious efficiency and charm. Its slightly off-kilter center field scoreboard is the last in the majors still operated by hand, yet it is only one that gives inning-by-inning scores of all out-of-town games. The roof is held up by a rusted network of rafters, a maze of horizontals and verticals and diagonals. Wrigley Field is a Peter Pan of a ballpark. It has never grown up, and it has never grown old."

– E.M. Swift
Sports Illustrated, 1980

The Wrigley Field scoreboard, built in 1937 at a cost of $100,000, requires three men to operate. Fenway Park's left-field scoreboard, built in 1933, usually houses two men. The Oakland Athletics have had a hand-operated scoreboard since 1986, and the Florida Marlins installed a hand-operated scoreboard prior to the 1993 season.

"To the serious Cub fan, the flags that matter above the scoreboard are the ones that represent the standings of the National League. The significance of them is not the standings -- a serious Cub fan looks at the standings before he looks at the bottom of his cereal bowl -- but the direction in which they whip as he approaches the ballpark."
– Lonnie Wheeler
  Bleachers, 1988

Flags of the 14 National League teams fly from yardarms in order of the standings on the morning of a game; the Eastern Division is to the west and the Western Division is to the east. The tradition of displaying the standings with flags was initiated in 1938 when there were just eight teams in the National League and no divisions. In 1969, the flagpole was replaced with a taller version to make room for expansion teams. In 1993, the flags were made a bit skinnier to accommodate the new clubs. The flagpole now rises 40 feet above the scoreboard.

"In the general area of promotion, Wrigley and I agreed on only one thing: keeping the park clean. My father had a phobia about a clean park. Phil Wrigley carried it even further; he made the park itself his best promotion... His solution (to boost poor attendance when the Cubs were losing) was to sell 'Beautiful Wrigley Field;' that is, to make the park itself so great an attraction that it would be thought of as a place to take the whole family for a delightful day...

We sold 'Beautiful Wrigley Field.' We advertised 'Beautiful Wrigley Field.' The announcers were instructed to use the phrase 'Beautiful Wrigley Field' as often as possible."

— **Bill Veeck, Jr.**
Veeck – As in Wreck, 1962

"I grew up spending many of my summer and weekend afternoons sneaking into, or trying to sneak into, Cubs Park. I tried everything from sliding down iced beer chutes (my pants never did dry that day) to slipping angelically into a church group."
– Ira Berkow, 1984
The New York Times
Sports of the Times

"Every time I go to Wrigley Field, I have memories of earlier times. They bring back good thoughts and energy."
    – Ernie Banks
        Cubs infielder, 1953-71

Homerun chasers on
Waveland Avenue
warm up during batting
practice.

"A baseball park, like Wrigley Field, is a place for play. A stadium is a site for gladiatorial extravaganzas, such as football."

— George Will

*"In this stream-
lined setting, every
wish of the patron
for comfort was
satisfied. Concession
Stands were above
what was consid-
ered standard in
other ballparks for
grandstands and
box seat patrons.
There was a blend-
ing of colors within
the field, which
enhanced the beau-
ty of the place."*
– Warren Brown
  The Chicago Cubs,
  1946

"Every player should spend a year with the Cubs to have fun in Wrigley Field."
– **Alvin Dark**
   Cubs infielder, 1958-59

"Wrigley Field in Chicago is a splendid argument against baseball chic."
– Roger Angell
Five Seasons

The ground crew is made up of 22 men. Five men are responsible for the condition of the playing field. The remaining 17 members handle the general upkeep and maintenance of the park.

"*I hate those magic carpets. The ball bounces around like a yo-yo. Just give me grass, daylight ball, and another pennant flying over Wrigley Field.*"
– Bill "Swish" Nicolson
  Cubs outfielder,
  1939-48

The infield slopes four inches from the edge of the pitchers mound to the edge of the infield dirt. From center field, the outfield slopes 10 inches to each foul pole.

The infield grass is 1 1/2 to 2 inches long, and the outfield grass is 2 inches long. The entire field was resodded in 1949 and 1960. In 1983, Kentucky bluegrass was planted to replace the diseased Merion bluegrass.

"It's a close park -- you have eye contact with people -- you cannot hide anything. It's like being under a microscope."
— Ernie Banks
Cubs infielder, 1953-71

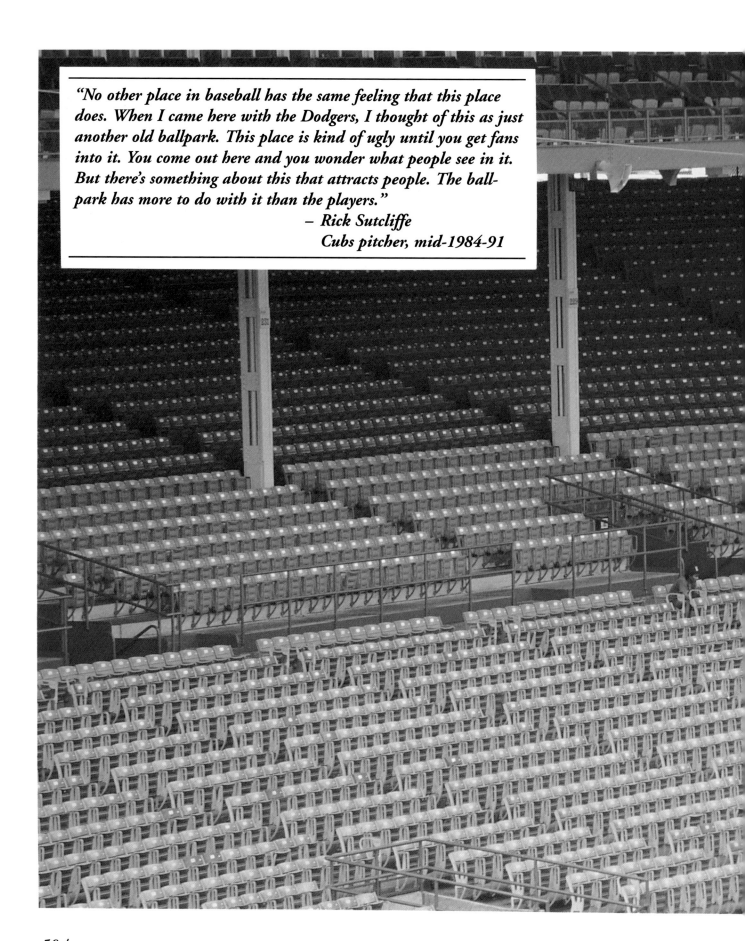

"No other place in baseball has the same feeling that this place does. When I came here with the Dodgers, I thought of this as just another old ballpark. This place is kind of ugly until you get fans into it. You come out here and you wonder what people see in it. But there's something about this that attracts people. The ballpark has more to do with it than the players."
– Rick Sutcliffe
Cubs pitcher, mid-1984-91

"The stands, so far as the spectator is concerned, will be as fit as any in these parts... seats will be afforded nearly 20,000 fans, 18,000 being in the grandstand. Only one bleacher has been erected, and this will nearly seat 2,000 'two-bit' fans... An enormous space has also been set aside for automobiles."

– **Handy Andy**
Chicago Tribune, April 1914
(after preseason tour of Weeghman Park)

"*The outward view from the catwalk is felicitous and hopeful: the converging faraway left-field and left bleacher sections complete the lines of the ancient vessel that plows forever dead ahead into Waveland and Sheffield Avenues, while the bleachers in center rise bravely toward the prow of the great green scoreboard, topped by a single lofty mast, its rigging aflutter with signal pennants (the current standings, top to bottom, of the teams in the two National League divisions), which customarily tell of happier news in other places.*"
— Roger Angell
"*Fortuity*" midsummer 1986

"Ballplayers come and go, but Wrigley Field endures. As long as Cub fans take their kids out to the Friendly Confines and show them where baseball should be played, the chain will be unbroken."

— Ernie Banks
Cubs infielder, 1953-71

"This is a great place. A kid's ballpark. Parents have been sending their kids to this park for decades for a number of good reasons. It's accessible, it's clean, it's safe, it's beautiful and it's baseball."
– Cotton Bogren
    Wrigley Field Groundskeeper 1925-82

The Treasury of Remembrance

By Roger Kahn
Author, *Boys of Summer*

In a rare 40-year-old book, the National League ballparks march before my view, pale elephants stirring against a vanished dawn. Each is carefully diagrammed by section. Dotted lines indicated distances to the walls. A few words of description speak quietly.

Polo Grounds, New York, New York. Double-decked stands. Bleachers. Capacity 55,000.

Forbes Field, Pittsburgh, Pennsylvania. Double-decked stands. Three tiers of boxes. Bleachers. 34,249.

Ebbets Field, Brooklyn, New York. Double-decked stands. Bleachers covered. 31,902.

They are all gone now and so is Crosley Field and Sportsman's Park and Connie Mack Stadium. Not one stone stands. The Roman Colosseum, completed in 80 A.D., remains in stirring ruin, but the National League ballparks of the 1950s, each in its way a shrine, have been shattered by the wrecker's ball. Odd when you think of it. We are a nation consumed by nostalgia. We weep beery tears at even banal mentions of the past. But the buildings, the shrines, what happens to American shrines?

Hey, Mac. We got this leveraged real estate deal. We flatten the damn park. We put up Elysian Fields Apartments. Then we take the profits and buy Cleveland, or maybe Fort Myers. Yeah, Fort Myers.

Better weather there and a cleaner beach.

Wrigley Field is widely admired today because it deserves to be admired. But surely some of the passion it produces traces simply to survival. Along with Fenway Park, in Boston, it is the patriarch of major league ball yards, the last of an endangered species. These old parks were not built on freeways; there were no freeways, nor was there even such a word so many years ago. They stood and stand in neighborhoods. Baseball is a populist game and you could reach the old parks by public transportation, subways, "Els," and trolley cars. Inside, you looked out beyond the bleachers and saw parts of a city. Brooklyn, Pittsburgh, Chicago. You knew where you were. Try that in the wretched modern cement coffee cups that try to pass for a stadium today.

I heard of Wrigley Field first in portraits articulated by the famous Dodger broadcaster, Red Barber. Sportsman's Park, St. Louis, was "the only big league ball park west of the Mississippi River." I heard that again and again. Wrigley Field was always "Beautiful Wrigley Field." Not the Friendly Confines. "Beautiful Wrigley Field." Barber waxed poetic about the brick outfield wall and the greenery that adorned it.

As an urban child I found myself mystified. Ivy on outfield walls? What happened when a line drive carried deep? Crushed leaves? Mashed stems? Green soup? And as an urban sandlotter, I wondered about caroms.

I first visited Wrigley Field for myself in 1952, and abruptly felt disappointment. It was April. A cold April. The walls were bare. No ivy was in leaf. And the wind. Why hadn't the Old Redhead told me about the wind? I sat through nine unremarkable innings, shivering.

Do you remember the old movies in which a secretary looks homely until a final scene when at long last she takes off her spectacles? Homely? That's no homely secretary, man. That's the beauteous blond bombshell, Lana Turner.

Ever since that first visit, Wrigley Field has been taking off its glasses for me. I came to appreciate the dimensions, just about right, 400 feet to center field. I came to like the intimacy, with the stands so close to the playing area that fans are almost in the game. And the wind. I even got to appreciate the wind. Someone has calculated that the wind blows in 52 percent of the time; blows out 31 percent of the time (and blows across the field twelve days out of a hundred). The wind offers variety; it changes the dimensions, so to speak. I once watched Duke Snider hammer three terrific smashes to right center off the Cubs' sturdy righthander, Warren Hacker. A strong wind blew in from Lake Michigan, and Frankie Baumholtz collared every smash. "Damn gale," Snider says to this day. "If it was going the other way, I'd a hit home runs."

I came to enjoy the park and the ivy and the press saloon called the Pink Poodle, where I heard baseball stories from Phil Cavaretta, Stan Hack, "Jolly Cholly" Grimm and even from the late, fanciful orator, Leo Durocher. I liked these things, and enjoyed these people, but before passion for a ballpark truly grips your innards, you have to see one great game there. Not good or exciting. A great ball game, that belongs to the ages.

In 1970, when I was contributing monthly

stories to *Esquire Magazine*, Bob Gibson, the wonderful Cardinal pitcher, telephoned one winter afternoon and said he had a good idea for the subject of an article. Bob Gibson. I agreed and we immediately made a date to meet on opening day. (In those days, there was no question who would pitch opening day for St. Louis.) Gibson was strong, brave, verbal and intimidating when situations called for intimidation. He had come from wretchedly poor beginnings in Omaha and he'd fought a fine struggle against racism for years.

"I hope you win the ball game, Bob," I said, fervently, and I meant it. Gibson hated losing and I was looking forward to a pleasant day and a happy dinner after he pitched.

April 6, 1971, in Chicago was not particularly pleasant. The temperature stayed at 40 degrees. Steam rose from the coffee cups fans clutched in the chill. Still the game sold out by 10:45 a.m. They announced the crowd at 42,121. People wore stocking caps and hoods and parkas and said, "Boy, it's a cold day for baseball. Where's the flask?"

I sat in the press box, upstairs behind home plate. The Cubs started Ferguson Jenkins and the long right-hander held off a good Cardinal line-up. Lou Brock, Ted Sizemore, Joe Torre. Gibson was commanding. He pitched hitless ball for three innings. Then Billy Williams and Ron Santo singled. The Cubs scored a run when Johnny Callison hit a fast ball off his thumbs and dumped a pop fly double into right.

Jenkins held the Cardinals to two hits into the seventh. Then a fast ball drifted toward the middle of the plate and Torre cracked into the left-field bleacher. Tie game.

The two masters proceeded with their overpowering magic. I watched spellbound (and was secretly glad not to have to bat against either). In the last of the tenth inning, a familiar character dropped into the seat next to mine. "Change speeds," Stan Musial said. "The mound is in sunlight now and the plate is in shadow. It's tough for a hitter to pick up the baseball. Change speeds."

The game was still tied. Gibson was pitching to Billy Williams. He threw an inside fast ball for a strike. He missed with a let-up, changing speeds as though he had heard Musial. Coming off the let-up, Gibson threw a 90 mile an hour fast ball at the knees and Billy Williams hit the baseball into Lake Michigan. (Well, toward Lake Michigan anyway.) That was the ball game: Chicago 2, St. Louis 1, in a brisk 1 hour and 59 minutes.

"A pitching masterpiece," wrote George Langford in the *Chicago Tribune.* "Jenkins pitched the best game of his life. Gibson threw better than he had in years."

I took my time leaving Wrigley for the dinner date with Gibson. I wanted to savor this great game. I wanted *him* to get over this great game.

At the restaurant Gibson sat alone, except for a bottle of vintage Bordeaux. He growled, "You're late. Where the hell have you been?"

"I didn't think you'd want to talk right away after losing one like that."

Gibson looked exasperated. "Did you come out here to work, or mess around?" He then spoke with profound intensity. Across the years, he'd read hundreds of stories in which a pitcher lost because of a mistake -- a hanging curve, a belt high fast ball. But that was not what happened today.

"I pitched Billy Williams the way I wanted to pitch him," said Gibson, proud, and defiant. "I made just the pitch I wanted to make." The visage softened. "Point that out in your story. This is the major leagues and in the major leagues, even good pitches get hit."

"That's what you saw today..."

I had also seen my great game. Passing Wrigley Field ever since, I don't think of ivy or public transportation.

I think of Fergie Jenkins and Stan Musial and Billy Williams and Bob Gibson, dauntless in chilly April, all winners, all golden in the treasury that is remembrance.

"The fences in the power alleys are so close, you're certain the next man will hit a homer; you're so close to the umpire that you can hear him cough; and suddenly the crowd decides it will sing a song. Wrigley Field is Great."
— **Thomas Boswell**
How Life Imitates the World Series

"*Baseball is a populist game -- you could reach the old parks by public transportation. ... Inside, you looked out beyond the bleachers and saw part of a city. Brooklyn, Pittsburgh, Chicago. You knew where you were.*"

– Roger Kahn

"Until they put those baskets on the outfield wall, it was an umpire's nightmare trying to decide whether or not the ball would have been a home run, because the fans in the front row could reach out towards the field and touch the ball."

– Doug Harvey
National League Umpire, 1962-92

This 42-inch wire basket in front of the bleachers was installed in 1970 to prevent items "misplaced by bleacher fans" from reaching the field. This required getting a waiver from league officials as there was a rule barring any change in field dimension after the season starts. Billy Williams was the first player to hit a home run into the basket, May 10, 1970. That same year, the Chicago Bears played their last football game at Wrigley Field.

The Cubs did not play the "Star-Spangled Banner" at all home games in 1948. "We feel that the playing of the National Anthem should not be a regular thing, but should be reserved for special occasions."

*"The greatest spot
in the world is
Wrigley Field in
Chicago because
there you have
afternoon baseball.
The game was
made to be played
in the daytime."*
– Shag Crawford
  National League
  Umpire, 1956-75

"An afternoon at Wrigley is the greatest buy in the country. It's sitting in the sun, drinking a few beers and telling a few lies. You can't beat the price or the entertainment."
– Bill Veeck, 1984

"For the fans, there never was any place to compare with Wrigley Field. All parks should be like that, and the people there were something special. They came to sit in the sun and watch baseball, not to boo the players."
— **Frankie Baumholtz**
Cubs outfielder, 1949-55

"Wrigley Field is one of the few remaining enclosures that still merit the title 'ballpark' -- a grassland enclosed by an ancient red brick wall and a gentle, curving, spacious sweep of stands, two levels high along the foul lines, that is surmounted by a low, shadowy pavilion roof. Unlike many of the surviving original stadiums, the place is handsomely tended and painted..."
— **Roger Angell**
Five Seasons

"Face it, this is a Cub town and has been for more than half a century, not because the Cubs have had the better or worse team, but because of Wrigley Field, which is an absolute treasure."

– Jerome Holtzman
Chicago Tribune, 1986

Once a Cub Fan...

By "Dutch" Rennert
National League umpire, 1973-92

In my twenty years umpiring in the National League, I have spent many happy afternoons in Wrigley Field. What a great place to umpire in! And I love daytime baseball.

Whenever I work Wrigley Field, I look beyond center field and out into the bleachers. My mind goes back to when I was an 11-year-old fan and sat out in those same bleachers. I was born and raised in Oshkosh, Wisconsin, 153 miles from Chicago. I used to listen to Cubs games on the radio and tried to imagine "beautiful Wrigley Field" that the announcers were talking about. It was always my big dream to visit Wrigley Field and see the Cubs play. But 153 miles was a long trip back then and my father was a working man, and couldn't get the time off his job to take me to a game. Some folks think I'm stubborn now, and I guess I was stubborn then, because I made up my mind that I'd go by myself. There was just one thing wrong with that idea -- I didn't have dad's permission...

I walked out to Highway #41 -- remember I was 11 years old -- and stuck out my thumb and hitch-hiked all the way to Wrigley Field. Now *that's* a Cubs fan.

As you might guess, my family was worried and reported me missing -- their boy, a run-away. Although I had slipped away without telling my parents, I had bragged about my plans to everyone else in Oshkosh. When my parents became worried, someone must have let them in on my secret. The next day I'm back at Wrigley Field, enjoying my second Cub game, when a couple of Chicago police officers pick me up and put me on a train back to Oshkosh.

Needless to say, my dad was very upset. But underneath the anger and worry he really understood. He was a Cub fan himself, and once a Cubbie fan, always a Cubbie fan. So even after hundreds of games at Wrigley Field, I still love the place. I especially love those games when I'm working behind the plate -- I can look out into those center-field bleachers, think of my childhood and thank the Lord I'm an umpire. I've got the best view in the park and didn't have to pay to get in!

"*Cub fans, by consensus are the best in baseball. Year after year, in good times and (mostly) bad, they turn out in vociferous numbers, sustaining themselves with heavenly ichor that combines loyalty, criticism, cheerfulness, durability, rage, beer and hope, in exquisite proportions.*"
                    – Roger Angell
                    Season Ticket

"The obvious occurred to me. That a ballpark is, first of all, a park. Looking out over the outfield fences I saw a city neighborhood, but there, inside the boundaries, was parkland so beautifully tended and tranquil that it was almost jarring. No wonder people make a habit of going to baseball games even when their team is not doing particularly well."
– Bob Greene
Chicago Tribune,
1981

The ivy was still in bloom for the 1989 playoffs. However, according to the *Chicago Tribune*, had it turned brown, Cubs management would have considered spray painting it green.

"As thick as the ivy that hugs its red brick walls, the very essence of baseball hangs in the atmosphere of Wrigley. Not only the ballpark itself, with its vine-covered walls and hand-operated scoreboard, but the folks that grace the place are why Chicago's North Side park is the purest in baseball... Reminiscent of a day when life was simpler, it's the tiny neighborhood's love affair with baseball that makes the park so special."

– Bob Wood
Dodger Dogs to Fenway Franks, 1988

"An afternoon in the bleachers of Wrigley Field is the quintessential Chicago experience. Rapid-fire banter between vendors and customers, debates among fans and well-orchestrated jeering between the partisans of the right-field and left-field sections are the side show; the attraction is baseball, and it begins with the players taking their warm-ups within hailing distance. The crowd is a mixture of old-timers in straw hats and youngsters on vacation, suntans and braces identifying their social status. The girls wear halter tops and alligator-crested golf shirts; most of the boys are topless."

– Skip Rozin
Audubon, 1984

On this day at the park, 38,242 fans consumed 28,504 hot dogs, 36,152 soft drinks and 39,769 beers.

"At Wrigley Field, a wave was graffi-ti. Starting one was like doodling in the family Bible or sticking gum on the wall of the Louvre."
– Bob Wood
   Dodger Dogs to Fenway Franks

"Wrigley Field stands as quite probably the best and surely the most beautiful place in the nation to watch baseball."
— Paul Gapp, architecture critic
Chicago Tribune

"The bleachers... where the scent of suntan oil, broiled hot dogs, and spilled beer creates a wondrous feeling of euphoria -- a feeling that neither crowds, hard benches, long ticket lines, nor the endless trek to distant toilets can diminish. The bleachers aren't just concrete and steel, cheap seats, and concession stands; they're a state of mind, a way of life, the best of summer."

– Bill Veeck
Chicago Magazine, 1984

The center-field bleachers were open to fans from 1937 through the 1940 season. They were closed from 1941 through 1947; they were opened again from 1948 through 1951. They were closed for good on April 20, 1952, following a series with the St. Louis Cardinals. Speaking with the press after a game at Wrigley Field, Stan Musial said, "When people are sitting in those middle sections of the bleachers, it's just impossible to follow the ball. The background is just plain murder, and that's just what it's going to result in one of these days if something isn't done." League officials made a special exception in 1962, allowing fans to sit in the center field section for the All-Star game. The center-field television camera, now used in every ballpark, was introduced at Wrigley Field in 1954.

"Our audiences are composed of the best class of people in Chicago, and no theater, church, or place of amusement contains a finer class of people that can be found in our grandstand."

– Albert G. Spalding
White Stockings owner, 1883

Upper photo: Blind fans frequent the right-field bleachers.

"There's more knowledge about baseball in these bleachers than in the whole rest of the park."
– Bill Veeck

"The Wrigley Field scoreboard in Chicago is the most imposing, towering more than a hundred feet above the center-field fence. It serves as the roof for some of the liveliest gamblers in the Midwest, who will lay odds that the next batted ball will fall into the first row of seats along third base and strike a blonde on her left wrist. In rain, snow, sunlight and smog, the Wrigley Field gamblers huddle near the scoreboard, a scene of togetherness in a frequently raucous and loudly individualistic bleacher crowd.

The clock atop the Cubs scoreboard has been two minutes slow for the last five years, and has its counterpart in the ball and strike operator, who is frequently one pitch behind the umpire. Closer attention is paid by the bullpen, however, to the posting of scores in other major league games. A blank panel in the board is replaced with a numbered panel. The speed with which this switch is made usually indicates whether or not a run has been scored in that particular half inning. Zeros are painted on the opposite side of the blank panels; number panels must be retrieved from stacks inside the scoreboard. Many a beer has been bet in the bullpen on how many runs will be posted to replace an empty panel. It's a split-second wager to be made only by experienced bettors."

— Jim Brosnan, Cub pitcher 1954-58
The Long Season, 1960

The metal scoreboard
number panels weigh five
pounds each and measure
15 1/2 inches by 20 inches.
The pitcher indicator numbers,
at the far left of the line
score, are 9 1/2 inches high
and 14 1/2 inches wide.

The clock atop the scoreboard was added in 1941. It is 10 feet in diameter and required a ton of steel to construct.

According to the *Chicago Tribune* in 1937, the ball and strike indicators, "embody ingenious new magnetic principles never before employed in scoreboard design." The ball and strike openings are 18 inches wide by 30 inches tall. Each is made up of eight rows of four-inch holes in the scoreboard. At the throw of a lever, "eyelids" are lifted from the appropriate openings, exposing the white panels beneath.

"The ivy, many would say, is what puts the ubiquitous adjective in Beautiful Wrigley Field. Actually, the bricks are underrated in that regard, but the ivy does look comelier every year in the lineup of polyester ballparks. Its loveliness is not only in its verdant complexion, but in the attitude it expresses, an appreciation of aesthetic virtue too often bygone in a sport of the heart."
– Lonnie Wheeler
   Bleachers, 1988

Wrigley Field: The Mayor's Office

By Hank Sauer, the "Mayor of Wrigley Field"

Cubs Outfielder, 1949-55
National League Most Valuable Player, 1952

I played in all the National League parks that were in use in the 1940s and 50s, and Wrigley Field was as good as or better than any of them. I came up to the major leagues with Cincinnati and we were playing in Crosley Field, which was a nice park at the time, but it was an old park, and had this tricky slope in the outfield. But, like I said, Wrigley was as good as or better than any of them then. And the thing that's really remarkable is that Wrigley Field is *still* as good as any park today. The playing field was always meticulously kept, and the park itself was cleaner than most. And the outfield ivy gave the park a beautiful appearance.

There was a certain camaraderie at Wrigley Field that didn't exist anywhere else -- a camaraderie not just between players but also between the players and the fans. They started calling me the "Mayor of Wrigley Field" in 1952 because I led the league in runs and tied for homers. In fact, every time I hit a home run, bleacher fans threw packets of chewing tobacco out on the field to me, which I mixed with chewing gum.

The fans in Wrigley Field were more knowledgeable about baseball than fans in other parks. They all cheered the good plays, no matter who made them, and I really can't remember them booing any particular player. That is with the exception of a player who was loafing on the field, and then they let him have it. Of course I never caught an earful of booing because I was always giving 100 percent.

As for the dimensions of Wrigley Field, a lot of people think of Wrigley Field as a small park, you know, easy to hit home runs in, but it really wasn't. In fact the dimensions were longer than a lot of other parks we played in then. If it was smaller in any way, it was the size of the foul territory. The stands were so close that it was almost impossible to "pop out" foul.

In 1959, after I had been traded to the Giants, we realized that someone was in the scoreboard stealing the signs our catcher was giving to the pitcher. Some fellow was up there and he'd put his foot up in the scoreboard opening to signal the Cub batter that the next pitch would be a fastball. He'd put both feet up if it was a curve, and he'd put one foot up in the middle of the ledge if it would be a change-up. We never actually saw their guy using a telescope or binoculars or whatever, but we knew they were doing it, and when we realized that they were stealing the signs, we tried our darndest to get up there and get that guy in the scoreboard. We never could prove it, but when that guy wasn't stealing our signs, the Cubs stopped hitting our pitchers. You might wonder if we ever did that when I was on the Cubs, but if they were, I wasn't aware of it. I suppose if we were doing it I would've hit even better.

"While it would be an exaggeration to suggest that time stops at Wrigley, evidence indicates it moves more slowly there... This quality is uniquely suited to baseball. More than any of our other sports, it does not bend to time or schedule. Things happen very quickly, then slowly, affording a fan the opportunity not only to enjoy the action, appreciating the talents of the athletes on the field, but to let his mind wander, to compare their skills with those of their predecessors."
– Skip Rozin
   Audubon, 1984

"After you learn all the angles in this park, you could probably become a good pool player... On any given day, those lovely ivy-covered walls can bring you to your knees."
– Keith Moreland
  Cubs infielder,
  1982-85

"In planning the construction of the new bleachers, (Wrigley) decided that an outdoor woodsy motif was definitely called for. Since I had always admired the ivy-covered walls at Perry Stadium in Indianapolis I suggested that we appropriate the idea for ourselves...I had planned on planting at the end of the season, after the bleachers had been completely rebuilt. By the time the new season came around, the ivy would have caught and Mr. Wrigley would have his outdoor atmosphere...The Cubs were ending the season with a long road trip, returning home only in the final week for one last series.

The day before the team was to return, Mr. Wrigley called me in to tell me that he had invited some people to the park to watch the game and gaze upon his ivy.

'Holy smokes,' I said, 'I haven't even ordered it yet, let alone planted it. But I'll see what I can do.'

John Seys, the vice president, called a friend who owned a nursery. He informed us that ivy couldn't be put in overnight.

'Well,' I said, 'what can I put in place of ivy?'

'Bittersweet,' he said.

Bob Dorr, the groundskeeper, and I strung lights all along the fence to enable us to work through the night. When the morning sun broke over the grandstand roof, it shone upon the bleacher wall entirely covered with bittersweet. We had planted the ivy in between and, in time, the ivy took over."

– Bill Veeck
Veeck - As in Wreck, 1962

"In person, Wrigley is the ivy! So much thicker than I ever imagined it to be, like a rich fur coat, it hugs the outfield wall. And the color -- not just green -- is a deep, dark green. The plant hypnotizes. It overrides everything inside. Wherever my eyes roamed, it wasn't long before they came back to rest on the outfield vines."

– Bob Wood
Dodger Dogs to Fenway Franks, 1988

"Wrigley Field is a ballpark. If there was one way to rile Philip K. Wrigley, the retiring gentleman who owned the Chicago Cubs between 1932 and his death in 1977, it was to refer to Wrigley Field as a stadium. It is a park, with spiders and grasshoppers and vines an inch around on the field of play. The vines come into bloom in mid-May. The morning glories open up pale blue and pink and purple and are shut again by noon. The greenish-white flowers of the bittersweet bloom inconspicuously against the ivy. There is Boston ivy with its eight-inch leaves that stick out from the brick a foot and a half and are clipped by the ground crew before every home stand. There is Baltic ivy with its shiny, leathery leaves that stay green all winter, and the high-climbing Virginia creeper, whose five-leaflet clusters turn reddish-orange in the fall. That is when the bunches of grapes hang purple on the grapevines and the bittersweet berries turn red, but in the spring there are flowers where the fruit will be."

– E.M. Swift
Sports Illustrated, 1980

"The ball field is a mystic creation, the Stonehenge of America. That is, the bases are a magic 90 feet apart. Think how often a batter is thrown out by half a step, compared to instances when he outruns a hit to shortstop. But artificial surfaces have lately changed the nature, if not the dimensions of the diamond. A ground ball at Riverfront Stadium moves much faster than the same grounder bouncing on the honest grass of Wrigley Field..."

– Roger Kahn

"When we have the money, we'll probably install synthetic grass. There's no doubt it would pay for itself in a few years."

– P.K. Wrigley

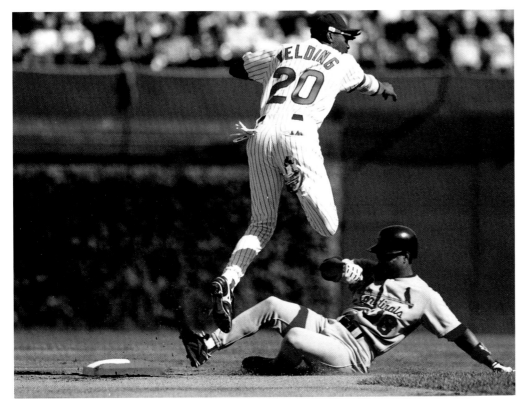

"I can't believe the view you get from here. Now I understand why fans keep coming out here."
– Glenn Beckert
Cubs infielder,
1965-73

"Wrigley is the perfect stage. Standing at home plate one morning before a game this summer, I was struck by the visual grace of the empty park. Double-decked grandstands escort the foul lines nearly all the way in right and left fields before the top deck falls away, exposing the lower tier to the sun. The outfield wall begins in the corners, runs straight for a few yards, then dips in to accommodate the bleachers. Those open stands begin low at both ends and build gradually, higher and higher, one block of seats becoming two, until they form the base for the huge scoreboard..."

– **Skip Rozin**
Audubon, 1984

In 1988, 66 skyboxes were added, the last of the 18-inch wide wooden seats were removed and were replaced with plastic seats; a new pressbox, seen here, was added, along with press dining; upper deck box seats were added, along with a food court and veranda seating area.

After tremendous debate, lights were installed in 1988 at a cost of $5 million. The nine banks of lights were built to conform with the architectural feeling of the park. The electricity for each game costs approximately $600, depending on the game's duration. Regardless of the length of the game, however, the organ must be turned off at 9:50pm.

There were 6,852 consecutive day games played at Wrigley Field before the Cubs played their first night home game.

"One of the silliest but most wide-spread fallacies in baseball is that Wrigley Field is somehow responsible for the Cubs' difficulties. That playing baseball games outdoors in the summer sun will, by August, sap a professional athlete of his strength. This theory would be more acceptable if they were the Sahara Cubs and each player was stripped and bound in the sand before his turn at bat, but two hours in the Chicago sun -- half of which is spent in the dugout -- could not seriously tax a fat albino."
– E.M. Swift
   Sports Illustrated
   1980

In 1949, a new electronic scoreboard was added on the front of the left-field upper deck for the benefit of bleacher fans at a cost of $15,000.

"Wrigley's simple close confines offer up some of baseball's finest views... From almost anywhere inside you're right on top of the action... Facial expressions, grimaces of satisfaction and frustration personalize it. Not only is it intense to watch, but sounds and smells join in. The scent of the grass rises up from the field. The catcher's mitt pops with the smoke of a fastball. The bat cracks if it somehow manages to meet the ball. Even a helmet slammed against the dugout in frustration makes noise. Baseball is so much more real."

– Bob Wood
   *Dodger Dogs to
   Fenway Franks*

"This great park is dedicated to clean sport and the furtherance of our national game."

– Newspaper advertisement
Opening day, April 23, 1914

"I can't play in Wrigley Field because the left-field foul line isn't straight like it is in other parks, it's crooked" (He also refused to go near the vine-covered outfield walls due to a fear that it was poison ivy.)

– Lou Novikoff
"The Mad Russian"
Cubs outfielder, 1941-44

Reflections on Wrigley

By Jerome Holtzman
Chicago Tribune Columnist
National Baseball Hall of Fame
J.G. Taylor Spinks Award

Over the years people have asked me, "Isn't it boring covering the Cubs?"
I would ask what makes them think that? The response is always the same:

"Well, they are always losing," or words to that effect.

What they failed to understand was, win or lose, and despite a long run of second-division finishes, the Cubs were always exciting. They almost always outdrew the cross-town White Sox who generally had the stronger team. Since the days of the Black Sox, 84 years ago, Chicago has been a Cub town, mostly, I am convinced, because of day games and the location and charm of "Beautiful Wrigley Field."

The late Philip K. Wrigley, the Cubs' caretaker for five decades, didn't seem to know much about baseball. In his later years he was a borderline absentee owner. I saw him only a few times at Wrigley Field and never during a game.

Accused of disinterest, he insisted he kept close watch on the team and saw many of the games on television which, he said, offered a better view.

Every time Wrigley expressed this view, Bill Veeck, who was then operating the White Sox, would slap his thigh in amusement. What delighted Veeck was that Wrigley, in effect, was advising Cub fans to stay home and watch the game on television themselves.

When I began covering the Cubs they had three vice presidents--a trinity of John Holland, Charlie Grimm and "Pants" Rowland, all supposedly with equal authority. The vice presidents (and some of the veteran players) often insisted they knew Mr. Wrigley well, and said that he was keenly interested and involved with the club.

I recall one day when the Cubs were playing the Phillies. Peanuts Lowrey, who had played with the Cubs, was then a coach with the Phillies. After the game, when I went to the visiting clubhouse, Peanuts said to me, "Did you see the old man? He was at the game today. In the front row, next to the Cub dugout."

I went to the Cub clubhouse for confirmation. I asked Ernie Banks, Ron Santo and Billy Williams, one at a time, if they were aware Mr. Wrigley was at the game. They each said, yes, they had seen him.

I hurried to the press box and wrote my story, leading off not with who won or lost but with the fact that Mr. Wrigley was in attendance.

The next day John Holland called me into his office and told me my story was in error. Mr. Wrigley wasn't at the game. The man in the first row had been his cousin.

The first Cub game I covered was Opening Day, 1957. Warren Spahn, then with the Milwaukee Braves, won 4-1 with a 4-hitter. Over the years many of the games I have seen are blurred in my memory, lost in the fog of time. But I never forgot that '57 opener. The Braves' Johnny Logan got the big blow, a home run off Bob Rush, a tall right-hander. Rush had two of the Cub hits and drove in their only run with a double.

I broke in with the arrival of Holland, who functioned as the general manager, and Bob Scheffing, who was about to begin his maiden voyage as a big league manager. Both had been promoted from the Los Angeles Angels, the Cubs' Triple A farm team in the Pacific Coast League. Holland had a long tenure. Scheffing was fired a day or two after the '59 season ended.

But Wrigley didn't give Scheffing the boot because he did a poor job. The Cubs finished fifth that year, not bad considering that Bob Rush was their only rotation starter with more than one full season of major league experience. Scheffing was fired in an effort to take the headlines away from the White Sox who had won their first pennant in 40 years; the World Series opened in Comiskey Park the next day.

Then, as now, the Cubs were an enjoyable and somewhat carefree assignment. There was no pressure to win. But unlike today, there was no big money. The Cubs' annual aggregate revenue was probably less than $5 million. There was no bidding for free agents. Instead of strengthening the team, the meager profits were poured into ballpark maintenance, reinforcing the concrete, installing more comfortable seats, etc.

More than anyone, Wrigley understood the value of Wrigley Field. The players were transients. The ballpark was his lasting and most important asset. Wrigley dismissed the daily newspaper coverage as unimportant. He often said all that was necessary was a small advertisement, which sometimes was placed in the amusement section announcing: "Major League Baseball Today, 3 p.m., at Wrigley Field." The opposing team was seldom identified.

The press box was directly behind the plate, at what could be considered mezzanine level, a wonderful view. There were two rows, accommodations for about 25 writers. Measured by current standards it would be inadequate but there was no space problem. There were four Chicago newspapers, all of which had a "beat" writer. It wasn't until 10 or 15 years later that the scribes from the outlying districts and local radio and television reporters were allowed in the main box.

The press box was moved to the rear of the second deck, under the roof in 1988, during the remodeling for night games. The old press area and beyond--down the right and left lines--was converted into sky boxes. It's now a long climb to the press coop, which is five stories up.

Today most baseball writers get to the park three to four hours before game time. When I began covering baseball the competition wasn't nearly as intense. We didn't arrive until an hour, at the most, an hour and a half before the first pitch. There wasn't much in the way of pre-game interviews. Nor was there a rush to the clubhouse for post-game quotes. It was a much more leisurely pace.

I was never impressed with the flood of new ballpark construction in the '60s. The new stadiums struck me as antiseptic, nothing more than symmetrical, look-alike concrete saucers. Perhaps I shouldn't be immodest but from the beginning I contended that Wrigley Field and Fenway Park in Boston, which had the smallest seating capacity in their leagues, were the best ballparks.

Dallas Green, when he took over the Cubs after the 1981 season, had little, if any, appreciation of Chicago or Cub fans. All of Green's previous baseball experience was with the Philadelphia Phillies. Worse, he surrounded himself with 22 people whom he had hired from the Phillies' organization.

As Bill Brashler, a noted Chicago author, observed "Cub tradition oozes like sap from a maple tree." But Green didn't understand and made a tremendous blunder with his initial promotional campaign that featured the slogan "Building A New Tradition." He was unaware that the Cubs had a glorious tradition--nine pennants in a 39-year stretch, including a sequence of a flag every third year, from '32 through '38.

I recall telling Green that the Cubs were the only National League team that had played in the same city, without interruption, since the league was founded in 1876; that it was a franchise with a storied and rich history, certainly more so than his beloved Phillies who, from 1900 through 1979, had won only two pennants.

But I'll say this for Green. Eventually, he learned to appreciate the unique charm and beauty of Wrigley Field. During the battle for night baseball Green threatened to move the franchise to the suburbs. Some politicians, eager to land the Cubs, were willing to build a ballpark without charge. Green said he would agree on one condition: that the new ballpark would be an exact replica of Wrigley Field.

"Let me hear ya, good and loud!"

"It's just about the most beautiful ballpark in the world. I've seen a lot of them in my time, and not one comes close... (also) everyone who comes to the park says it's the best in baseball. And I've been to a lot of the major league parks, and I've never seen one better."
– Cotton Bogren
Groundskeeper,
1925-82

> *"Wrigley's bleachers is one of the rare places where people of my generation get along with youngsters."*
>
> – Bill Veeck, 1983

"*The won-lost flags are actually more indulgent than informative, because any Cub fan worth Rich Nye's resin bag knows what the boys have done before he starts home.*"
– Lonnie Wheeler
  Bleachers, 1988

"People remember their days at Wrigley Field. It's the same there; it never changes. And when you leave... you're still there."
— Ernie Banks
Cubs infielder, 1953-71

"The first time you see Wrigley at night, it feels like you just saw your second grade teacher in the supermarket."
– Michael Benson
Ballparks of North America, 1991

"There was only one promotional gimmick I ever got away with. Mr. Wrigley permitted me to install lights on top of the flagpole to let homeward-bound Elevated passengers know whether we won or lost that day. The flagpole was on top of the new scoreboard, and on its summit I put a crossbar with a green light on one side and a red light on the other. The green light told the El passengers we had won, the red that we had lost."

— Bill Veeck, Jr.
Veeck – As in Wreck, 1962

(Editor's note: newspaper accounts of the day report that the light colors were blue for a win and white for a loss.)

In 1978, the win/loss lights were moved to cane-shaped poles on the backside of the scoreboard.

One of a Kind

By Doug Harvey
National League umpire, 1962-92

Chicago is a town of great contrasts. No other city can boast such big city confidence and, in the same breath, such a rough and shady past. Consider: beautiful Lake Michigan and the Great Chicago Fire; two major league baseball teams, each as old as the league it is a part of, and the dreadful "Black Sox" scandal; the Sears Tower and "Boss" Daley; and then there is Wrigley Field.

"Wrigley Field!" Say it fast, with a bit of bark to it, and it summons up all the sounds of concessionaires hustling their goods. Say it even quicker and memories of public address announcer Pat Pieper, forever young and yet already gone, as his voice boomed out "Welcome to Wrigley Field -- Home of the Chicago Cubs." His staccato voice always reminded me that this ballpark was in a tough town, the town that gave birth to the Capone Era, and an entirely different way to celebrate St. Valentine's Day.

"Wrigley Field." Say it slowly...let it roll over the tongue and slip past the lips. Immediately it conjures a world of wonder; a greenness that starts behind home plate, travels out to and then climbs up and over the outfield wall... 1969 when the Cubs were a *lock* to win the pennant, only to see their hopes dashed during the final month of the season... Ernie, Fergie, Billy, Ron, Jody, and "Ryno." Who needs a last name?.. Ten managers for one team in the early sixties... Monstrous home runs... Late innings when we all struggled just to see the ball (that is B.L., Before Lights)... The Bleacher Bums sitting next to the only manually operated scoreboard in the National League... And, before they were banned, white-shirted fans in dead center field, making it almost impossible for the batter (or the home plate umpire) to see the ball...

Sit back and say it even more slowly - "Wrigley Field..." Memories flood the mind. To all the people who have never had the pleasure of attending a Cubs home game, these memories have been created by what they have seen on television, read about, or heard on the radio. The imagery of the media is good, but believe me, it doesn't do justice to the "Jewel of Addison & Clark."

Viewed from above, it must seem like the Great God of Baseball took an older section of Chicago and forcibly squeezed a field in amongst the brownstone homes. Beyond both outfield walls, there are two sidewalks, two lane streets, and even a small yard in front of every home facing the ballpark.

What other ballpark could be famous for such unique situations as people sitting on their rooftops watching Major League baseball; or fans out on Waveland Avenue waiting to chase home runs hit out of the park; or the fact that every game will be different, depending on the direction and force of the wind? These gusts and gales are so capricious they guarantee feast or famine for the batters. Wrigley Field is the only park I know where both the umpires and the players check the flags to see the direction the wind is blowing before the game starts.

You, with brick walls covered so majestically with tangled vine, are one of a kind! Yours is a matchless personality. I love your city, your fans, and you, Wrigley Field.

ST. LOUIS	AB	R	H	BI	BB	SO
Glikey lf	5	2	2	1	0	1
O Smith ss	5	0	2	0	0	0
Jefferies 1b	5	0	1	1	0	0
Lankford cf	3	0	0	0	2	1
Whiten rf	5	1	1	0	0	1
Zeile 3b	2	0	1	1	2	0
G Pena 2b	2	0	0	0	0	1
a-Alicea ph-2b	1	0	1	0	1	0
Pagnozzi c	4	0	1	0	0	0
Arocha p	2	0	0	0	0	1
Urbani p	0	0	0	0	0	0
b-Perry ph	1	0	1	0	0	0
Kilgus p	0	0	0	0	0	0
c-Brewer ph	0	0	0	0	0	0
d-Woodson ph	1	0	0	0	0	0
Murphy p	0	0	0	0	0	0
Lancaster p	0	0	0	0	0	0
TOTALS	36	3	10	3	5	5

CHICAGO	AB	R	H	BI	BB	SO
D Smith cf	5	1	1	1	0	1
Vizcaino 3b	4	1	1	0	0	2
Sandberg 2b	3	0	1	1	0	0
Yelding 2b	1	0	1	0	0	0
Grace 1b	4	0	0	0	0	0
May lf	3	0	1	0	1	0
Wilkins c	4	3	3	0	0	1
Sosa rf	4	3	2	2	0	0
Sanchez ss	4	0	3	3	0	0
Boskie p	2	0	0	0	0	0
Scanlan p	0	0	0	1	0	0
Myers p	0	0	0	0	0	0
TOTALS	34	8	13	8	1	4

St. Louis	111	000	000--3	10	1	
CUBS	021	012	02x--8	13	2	

a-walked for Pena in the 6th. b-singled for Urbani in the 6th. c-announced for Kilgus in the 9th. d-flied out for Brewer in the 8th.

E-Whiten (2), Sandberg (5), Boskie (1). LOB-St. Louis 11, Chicago 5. 2B-Gilkey (14), O Smith (10), Zeile (16), Sanchez 2 (6). 3B-Vizcaino (3). HR-D Smith (8) off Arocha, Sosa (12) off Lancaster, Gilkey (4) off Boskie. RBI-Gilkey (22), Jefferies (37), Zeile (27), D Smith (20), Sandberg (23), Sosa (35), Snachez 3 (12), Scanlan (1). CS-Jefferies (5), Yelding (1). S-Myers. SF-Scanlan. GIDP-Gilkey.

Runners left in scoring position--St. Louis 6 (Lankford, Whiten, Pagnozzi 2, Arocha, Woodson); CUBS 4 (D Smith 2, Wilkins, Boskie).

Runners moved up-O Smith, Pagnozzi, Sosa. DP-Chicago 2 (Wilkins and Sanchez), (Yelding and Grace).

St.Louis	IP	H	R	ER	BB	SO	NP	ERA
Arocha L,5-2	5 2/3	9	6	6	1	3	97	3.05
Urbani	1/3	0	0	0	0	1	4	8.18
Kilgus	1	1	0	0	0	0	13	0.00
Murphy	1/3	1	1	1	0	0	4	3.62
Lancaster	2/3	2	1	1	0	0	17	3.46

Chicago	IP	H	R	ER	BB	SO	NP	ERA
Boskie W, 1-0	5 2/3	5	3	3	3	5	105	4.70
Scanlan	2	4	0	0	1	0	37	3.86
Myers S, 22	1 1/3	1	0	0	1	0	29	1.82

Inherited runners-scored-Urbani 1-0, Lancaster 1-1, Scanlan 3-0, Myers 2-0. WP-Lancaster. Umpires-Home, Williams; First, West; Second, Pulli; Third, Darling. T-2:58. A-38,242.